CONTENTS

KU-675-932

WITHDRAWN FROM STOCK

PUTTING SCIENCE TO WORK

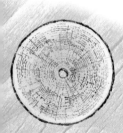

Using a scanning tunnelling microscope, which can move individual atoms, scientists have created an incredible new molecule. It is shaped like a propeller and is little more than a millionth of a metre across. When it is heated, the 'propeller' molecule starts spinning. One day, molecules like these will be put together to form micromachines as tiny as specks of dust.

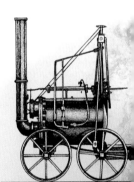

Rotating propeller-like molecules are some of the products being developed in one of the most exciting branches of modern technology – nanotechnology. It is called nanotechnology because scientists are working with objects – atoms – that are only nanometres across. A nanometre is a thousand-millionth of a metre.

Living with technology

Technology is the means by which we shape the world to suit us. It is often called applied science. Scientists discover things about our world, and technologists find ways of putting these discoveries to practical use. The scientist discovers while the technologist invents.

▲ Scientists have already taken the first steps in nanotechnology. This circular pattern was made by arranging individual atoms using a scanning tunnelling microscope.

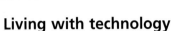

about 3500 BC
Wheel
The wheel first came into use in pottery-making. The first wagon wheels were wooden discs cut from tree trunks.

about 3500 BC
Plough
Farmers in the Middle East first used ploughs drawn by oxen for preparing the ground for sowing seeds.

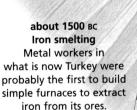

about 1500 BC
Iron smelting
Metal workers in what is now Turkey were probably the first to build simple furnaces to extract iron from its ores.

about AD 1050
Movable type
The Chinese began printing book pages using separate pieces of type made from baked clay. They could be used again and again.

1805
Steam engine
An early steam engine built by Englishman Richard Trevithick (1771–1883). He was the first engineer to use steam-power on a railroad.

1767
Spinning jenny
Invented by James Hargreaves (about 1720–1778) in England, this machine could spin threads on many spindles at the same time.

In technology, we take natural substances, such as clay and rocks, and transform them into materials that we can use, such as metals, fuels and chemicals.

With metals, we build magnificent structures like skyscrapers and suspension bridges, and machines to transport us and produce the goods we use. We burn fuels, such as oil and gas, in engines to power these machines or to produce electricity in power stations. We make all kinds of things with chemicals, from plastics and paint to medicines and make-up.

Good and bad

Technology can do great things. It can transform grains of sand into microchips, which are the brains behind our computers. It can build spacecraft that can travel billions of kilometres through the Solar System to visit far-distant planets. It can produce antibiotics to fight disease and cars that can travel faster than the speed of sound.

But technology is not all good news. To produce the materials and the machines we need, we are using up vast amounts of the Earth's natural resources, such as metals and other materials from rocks, and fuels such as oil and gas. These resources are limited and will one day run out.

Looking for answers

Technology is being used to try and solve some of the problems it has created. People in many countries are beginning to recycle some materials (use them again) instead of just throwing them away. Scientists are looking at new ways to obtain energy from the wind, waves and Sun because our main fuels – oil, gas and coal – are gradually running out. These alternative energy sources are renewable – they will not run out.

key words
- alternative energy
- fuels
- inventions
- nanotechnology
- pollution
- resources

▼ Some key inventions in the history of technology, from the wheel to the microchip. Technology developed rapidly after the 1700s.

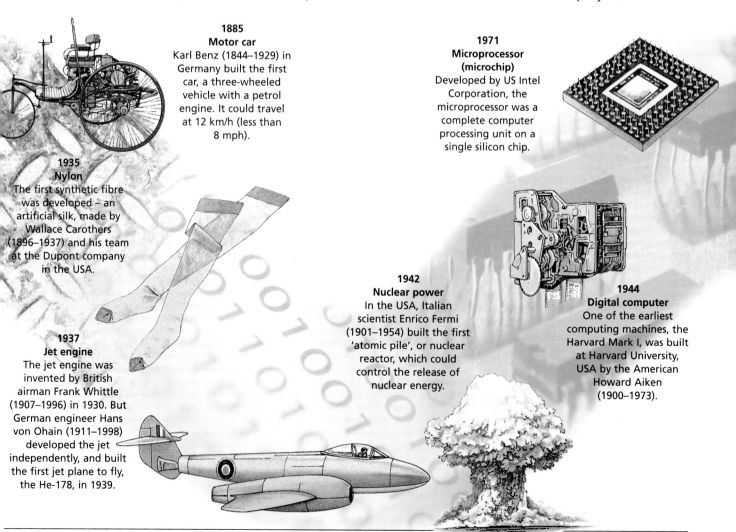

1885
Motor car
Karl Benz (1844–1929) in Germany built the first car, a three-wheeled vehicle with a petrol engine. It could travel at 12 km/h (less than 8 mph).

1971
Microprocessor (microchip)
Developed by US Intel Corporation, the microprocessor was a complete computer processing unit on a single silicon chip.

1935
Nylon
The first synthetic fibre was developed – an artificial silk, made by Wallace Carothers (1896–1937) and his team at the Dupont company in the USA.

1942
Nuclear power
In the USA, Italian scientist Enrico Fermi (1901–1954) built the first 'atomic pile', or nuclear reactor, which could control the release of nuclear energy.

1944
Digital computer
One of the earliest computing machines, the Harvard Mark I, was built at Harvard University, USA by the American Howard Aiken (1900–1973).

1937
Jet engine
The jet engine was invented by British airman Frank Whittle (1907–1996) in 1930. But German engineer Hans von Ohain (1911–1998) developed the jet independently, and built the first jet plane to fly, the He-178, in 1939.

THE TOOLS WE USE

Human beings are one of the few animal species that can make and use tools. Without tools, we could not easily farm the land, build houses or make a whole range of things. The tools that early humans used were made of readily available materials, such as stone, wood and bone. But most of the tools we use today are made of metal or plastic.

In their work and at home, people use hundreds of different tools for shaping and cutting materials, and fastening things together. They use knives, scissors and saws for cutting, hammers to knock in nails, drills to make holes, planes and files to smooth surfaces, and screwdrivers and spanners to tighten screws and nuts.

Today, many of these are power tools, which are driven by an electric motor. Some power tools operate from mains electricity, others are cordless and run on batteries.

▼ Some common hand tools used around the home. Using electrical power takes the hard work out of drilling holes and tightening screws.

THE FIRST TOOLS

Early humans first began using tools more than 2 million years ago, when they picked up handy-sized pieces of stone to chop and hammer things. In time they began deliberately shaping stones into tools like this flint hand-axe. Flint was a favoured material because it could be shaped easily to give a sharp cutting edge.

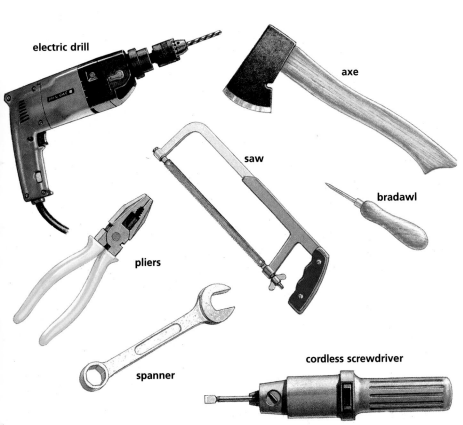

electric drill

axe

saw

bradawl

pliers

spanner

cordless screwdriver

Machine tools

In industry, huge power tools are used to cut and shape metal. They are called machine tools, and the work they carry out is called machining.

Machine tools hold the key to modern manufacturing because they cut very accurately and can produce parts that are a standard size. Many products, such as engines, are manufactured by fitting together sets of standard-sized parts on an assembly line.

In many workshops, machine tools are operated manually by engineers. But in large factories they usually work automatically, under computer control.

The cutting edge

Machine tools cut metal, which is very hard, so they must be harder still. Cutting tools are made from steel mixed with metals such as tungsten and chromium. Tungsten tools stay hard even when they get red-hot.

turning

milling

drilling

Tools get hot because of the friction between them and the metal piece they are shaping, which is called the workpiece. To reduce the friction, a watery oil is run over the tool. This cutting oil also helps to cool down the tool.

▲ Three of the most important machining processes are turning, milling and drilling.

Turning, drilling and milling

Three common machining operations are turning, drilling and milling. Turning is carried out on a lathe. The lathe rotates the workpiece, while tools are moved in to cut it. Lathes are used, for example, to cut the threads on screws.

A drill grips and turns a bit, which drills holes in the workpiece. A number of different-sized bits may be mounted on a movable holder so that they can be brought into action one by one.

A milling machine cuts slots and grooves in a metal surface. It uses a toothed cutting wheel that spins round. The wheel makes a cut as the workpiece moves beneath it.

Chemicals and sparks

Machine tools shape metal by cutting and grinding. But there are other ways to shape metal. In chemical machining, metal is etched (eaten) away by chemicals. In spark machining, high-voltage electricity is used to create a spark on the metal surface. The spark gradually wears the metal away.

◀ Sometimes machine tools work on a huge scale. For example, whole aircraft wings can be made by milling one enormous slab of metal. A wing made of a single piece of metal is much stronger than one made up of many bits joined together.

● key words

- automation
- flint
- lathe
- machining
- workpiece

MAKING THE GOODS

Two workers stand on either side of a car production line. A conveyor moves a partly built car between them. They pick up a wheel and fix it to the front axle with nuts. They pick up another wheel and fix it to the rear axle. Then another car comes by, and they repeat the process.

This way of working is called an assembly line. A product is made (assembled) from a series of parts added in turn. Different workers carry out different stages of the assembly. Because each worker carries out the same simple action all the time, he or she can do the job quickly.

Mass production

Assembly lines are widely used in industry to manufacture goods – anything from matches to aircraft. Manufacturing literally means 'making by hand'. But most goods today are machine-made in factories.

Making large quantities of goods using machines and assembly lines is much cheaper than making things by hand. The process is called mass production.

Automation

Some of the key machines used in industry are machine tools – machines that can make identical parts. If the parts are the same, they will fit together and the products can be made on an assembly line.

In many industries machines work automatically, controlled by a computer. For example, a computer may control a laser cutter that cuts a machine part from a sheet of metal. Where a number of machines need to work on a product in turn, it is automatically transferred from one machine to the next. This is called automation.

In 1913, US car manufacturer Henry Ford (1863–1947) began using moving conveyors on assembly lines. The time needed to make a car chassis (basic frame) was cut from 12 hours to 1½ hours.

▲ Today robots may work on assembly lines alongside people. These are not the human-like robots we call androids, but machines with mechanical arms that can move and grip things in the same way as human arms and hands. They often do the dirty jobs, like welding and paint spraying.

REVOLUTION IN INDUSTRY

Until about 250 years ago, most goods were made at home and sold locally. We call this kind of industry a cottage industry. But then people invented machines that speeded up spinning and weaving. In 1771, Richard Arkwright in England put many of these machines in a building and employed people to operate them. It became the first factory. Other people followed suit. At much the same time James Watt improved the steam engine, which then went into widespread use to power the factory machines. A revolution in working methods had begun, which we call the Industrial Revolution.

key words

- assembly line
- automation
- factory
- machine tool
- robot
- service industries

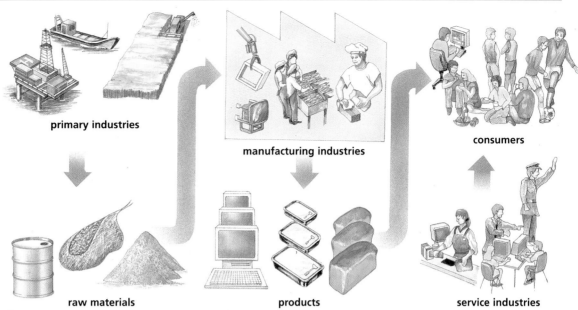

▶ Primary industries produce raw materials such as oil, fish and wheat. Secondary industries make the raw materials into products that people (consumers) use.

primary industries

manufacturing industries

consumers

raw materials

products

service industries

Primary and secondary

Manufacturing industries take raw materials, such as oil, rocks, wood or crops, and transform them into things such as fuels, metals, furniture and food.

The industries that provide these raw materials are known as primary industries. Mining, farming, forestry and fishing are all primary industries.

Manufacturing industries make use of materials that the primary industries provide. They are known as secondary industries. Some industries make products that we buy, but others, such as the chemical industry, make materials that are sold to other manufacturers.

At your service

After the goods have been produced, they have to be sold. The industries that sell the products of manufacturing are known as tertiary industries. They are also called service industries, because they provide a service to consumers (the people who buy and use the products). Shops and supermarkets are service industries.

Any business that provides a service to the public is known as a service industry. Examples include banking, nursing and information technology (work with computers).

As manufacturing industries become more automated, they provide fewer jobs for people. Gradually, more and more people are working in the service industries.

▼ Molten steel pours from a furnace. Made from iron, steel is by far the most important metal used in industry to build machines and structures.

WORKING ON THE LAND

In the vast prairie wheat fields of North America, it is harvest time. A convoy of combine harvesters is advancing through the golden grain, cutting swathes 10 metres wide. By the end of the day each one will have harvested 200 tonnes of wheat.

Today, the world is producing more food than ever before. Yet in countries such as the USA and UK only 2 per cent of working people farm the land. In these countries farming has become an efficient industry. Farmers make use of the latest research into growing crops and raising animals. And they use machines such as tractors, ploughs and combine harvesters to do much of the work.

People in some countries, however, still farm in traditional ways. One common method is shifting cultivation. Farmers clear land by cutting down and burning the vegetation. Then they plant their crops. After a few years, the soil becomes too poor to grow crops, and the farmers move on, leaving the land to recover.

Cultivating crops

Farmers grow all kinds of crops, including cereals, vegetables, fruit and nuts, sugar, oil, tea and cotton. Different crops grow best in different climates.

Cereals, such as wheat, rice and maize (corn), are by far the most important crops. They provide the staple (basic) food for most people.

Improved crop varieties are being introduced all the time. These may produce a bigger crop or give greater resistance to disease. Scientists produce new varieties by careful breeding.

▲ A water buffalo pulls a plough in a waterlogged rice paddy field in South-east Asia. Modern machinery would be of no use in such conditions.

key words

- cereal
- crop
- factory farming
- fertilizer
- livestock

▶ Combine harvesters cut cereal crops such as wheat and barley. The machine separates the grain from the stalks, then binds the cut stalks (straw) into bales.

Many farmers use chemicals to increase crop production. They add fertilizers to the soil, and spray their crops with pesticides and herbicides. Pesticides kill insects that attack the crops, and herbicides kill weeds. The problem with these chemicals is that they can harm other wildlife. Organic farmers avoid using such chemicals, and produce their crops using only natural fertilizers and pest control methods. There is an increasing demand for organic food in many countries.

Recently, scientists have started to use genetic engineering techniques to alter the genes of plants. This produces what are called GM (genetically modified) crops. Genetically modified crops can be made resistant to common pests or diseases. But many people are worried that they may also have harmful effects on the environment.

Raising livestock

Raising cattle is perhaps the most important kind of livestock farming. Beef cattle are raised for their meat, and dairy cattle for their milk. Friesian cattle can produce as much as 6000 litres of milk a year. Sheep, pigs and chickens are also important livestock.

Outdoors and indoors

Most livestock are raised outdoors either in fenced fields or on the open range. Farmers in North America and Australia have the biggest open-range farms, or ranches, where they raise beef cattle and sheep in vast numbers.

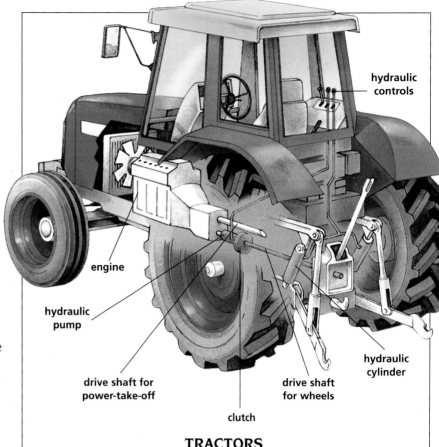

TRACTORS

A tractor can be used to drive all kinds of farm machinery, using power taken from the engine. The engine also powers a hydraulic (liquid pressure) system for lifting and lowering machinery. This cutaway drawing shows how the engine provides turning power (orange) and hydraulic power (green) to the back of the tractor.

Some livestock are raised by what are called factory farming methods. They are kept indoors under controlled conditions. Pigs and chickens are often farmed in this way. Factory farming produces meat and eggs cheaply, but many people think that it is cruel.

CROPS				LIVESTOCK			
rice	sugar	coffee	cotton	cattle	sheep	pigs	goats
top producing countries							
China India	India Cuba	Brazil Colombia	China USA	India	Australia	China	China (meat) India (milk)
world production							
520 million tonnes	120 million tonnes	5 million tonnes	20 million tonnes	1200 million	1100 million	800 million	450 million

PRINTING WORDS AND PICTURES

There was a time when all books were made of paper and words were printed on the pages. But no longer. Electronic books are now available that you read on a book-size screen. At the touch of a fingertip, you can change the size of the letters, put in a bookmark, make notes or look up words in the built-in dictionary.

Books printed on paper will still be with us for a long time. But methods of producing them are becoming increasingly electronic. Not so long ago, authors wrote their text (words) with a typewriter. Mistakes were marked on the paper copy, then a typesetter set the text in metal type (the lettering used in printing). Finally, a printing plate was made from the type.

Today, most authors write their text using a word-processor program on a computer. They send it to their editors on computer disk or by email. It may stay in electronic form through all the editing and design stages, until it gets to the printer, who makes the printing plates from an electronic file.

Scanning the pictures

Illustrations to go with the text are also stored in an electronic form. Professional photographers are increasingly using digital cameras, and many artists produce

▶ A page from one of the first and one of the most beautiful books ever printed, the Latin Bible made by German Johann Gutenberg (about 1400–1468). He printed it in about 1455, using movable metal type.

key words

- colour separation
- litho
- scanner
- type
- word processor

their artwork on a computer using illustration software. Photographs and illustrations on paper are converted into electronic form by a scanner.

A scanner works by scanning a laser beam across every part of a picture. This process records information about the colour and intensity of each tiny section of the picture in electronic form. When the

(a) (b) (c) (d)

◀ The four stages in printing a colour picture. The yellow plate is printed first (a), followed by the cyan plate (b), then the magenta (c). The black plate prints last, producing the full-colour picture (d).

picture is printed, this information is converted into patterns of dots for printing. Pictures have to be printed as tiny dots. You can see these dots if you look closely at a printed photograph in a newspaper or a book.

With a colour picture, four separate scans are made to produce four different images: one yellow, one cyan (blue), one magenta (red) and one black. This process is called colour separation. It depends on **the principle that any colour can be made** up from a combination of the colours **yellow, cyan and magenta. Printing plates** are made from these separations. (The fourth, black plate improves the look of the final picture.)

Printing processes

In the oldest printing method, called **letterpress, raised letters were coated with** ink and then pressed against a sheet of paper. Most printing now is done by a method called offset lithography (litho).

image on plate

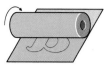
roller wets plate

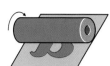
inking

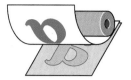
inked type transferred to paper

◀ In litho printing, a flat plate carries the type image. A roller wets all the plate except for the image, then another roller spreads ink, which sticks only to the type area. The inked image is then transferred to paper.

High-speed litho printing presses, fed by a continuous supply (web) of paper, can print 1000 copies every minute.

In litho printing, an image of everything to be printed in a particular colour is transferred photographically to a printing plate. The image is then treated so that sections that need to be dark attract greasy printing ink.

On the printing press, the plate is clamped to a cylinder, then wetted and inked in turn. The image areas repel the water but attract the ink. The cylinder revolves and transfers the ink image via another cylinder to the paper.

PRODUCING A MAGAZINE ARTICLE
A reporter and a photographer are covering a fire. This is the story of how technology helps to turn their words and pictures into a magazine article.

4 Magazine editors check finished page layouts produced by colour printer.

3 Designer designs pages of article on computer using text and photographs.

2 Photographer takes pictures to go with story and sends them via an ISDN line (fast telephone link).

1 Reporter records story on tape, types it up and emails it to magazine office.

5 Pages sent to printer as electronic files, which printer uses to make printing plates.

GUNS, BULLETS AND BOMBS

A cruise missile appears from nowhere flying only 20 metres or so above the ground along the city streets. It turns this way and that to miss the tall buildings. Then it homes in on its target, a bridge across the river, and blows it to smithereens.

Cruise missiles are frightening weapons. They can be launched at targets more than 2,000 kilometres away and hit them spot on. They can be launched from the ground, from ships or from aircraft. They fly low and are therefore difficult to detect by radar.

Cruise missiles are one of the many kinds of missile used by armed forces. Most missiles carry a high-explosive charge, which explodes when they hit their target. Some are fitted with nuclear warheads.

▲ An Apache helicopter of the US Air Force is a formidable fighting machine. It carries twin pods of rockets to attack ground targets and guided missiles for air-to-air combat.

key words
- artillery
- bombs
- firearms
- guidance system
- guns
- nuclear weapons

Power and guidance

Missiles are usually powered by rockets. The cruise missile is an exception. It has a jet engine. Most missiles are powered for all their flight. But ballistic missiles are powered only for the first part of their flight. Then the engine cuts out and they fall on to their target. The largest, intercontinental ballistic missiles (ICBMs) have a range of up to 10,000 kilometres.

Most missiles are guided to their target. Some lock on to radar signals from the target, or heat that the target gives out. Others carry TV cameras. Cruise missiles have a very accurate guidance system. It keeps them on a pre-set course following a detailed map of the ground held in an on-board computer.

Guns and artillery

A great many other weapons are used by fighting forces. Many of these are guns. The smaller hand guns are usually known as firearms; the bigger ones are called artillery. Pistols, revolvers, and rifles all fire small metal bullets, which are propelled · from the gun barrel by a small explosive charge. Rifles are so called because they have a spiral groove (rifling) in the barrel.

◄ This missile launcher is small enough to be fired by hand. It is firing an anti-tank missile.

▶ Laser bombing ensures great accuracy. A plane illuminates the target with a laser beam (a). Sensors in the bombs detect the beam and follow it down to the target (b).

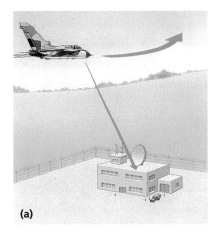 

(a)   (b)

This makes the bullet spin round, which helps it to travel straight.

Big guns (artillery) fire shells filled with high explosive, which explode when they land. Artillery can be used to bombard targets many kilometres away.

Bombs

Bombs are explosive weapons dropped from aircraft. They are fitted with fins so that they travel straighter in the air.

There are several types of aircraft bomb. Incendiary bombs are designed to destroy by fire. They are made of materials such as magnesium, which burns brilliantly. Armour-piercing bombs have a thick, hard nose to break through the armour on ships and tanks, for example.

Chemical and germ warfare

Some weapons are specifically designed to kill people rather than destroy buildings and equipment. Chemical weapons include gases like chlorine, mustard gas and nerve gas. Nerve gases are particularly deadly. They are absorbed through the skin, and can kill in minutes. Bacteriological weapons use deadly germs such as anthrax to kill people. Chemical and germ weapons are banned under international agreements, but many countries still have them.

THE ULTIMATE WEAPON

The most deadly weapons of all are nuclear weapons. They can destroy whole cities and their inhabitants in an instant, and the radiation from a weapon can cause death and sickness in an area for many years. The biggest have the destructive power of millions of tonnes of ordinary high explosive. There are two kinds of nuclear weapon. In atomic bombs, huge amounts of energy are released when atoms split – this process is called fission. In hydrogen bombs, another process called nuclear fusion is used which releases even greater destructive power.

▼ Modern automatic assault rifles like this Kalashnikov AK47 are capable of firing at a rate of up to 800 rounds a minute. Some of the gas released when a round is fired drives back the bolt ready to fire another round.

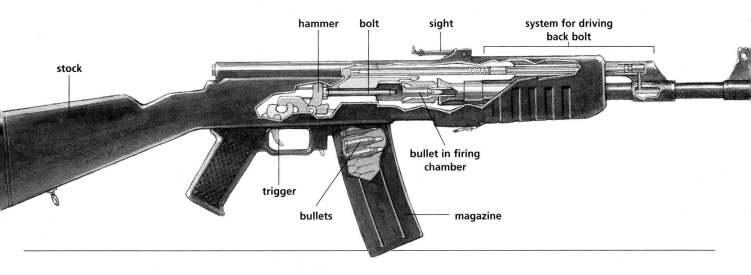

stock

hammer   bolt   sight   system for driving back bolt

bullet in firing chamber

trigger

bullets   magazine

BUILDING WORKS

For thousands of years humans have been changing the face of the Earth to make their lives easier. They have built houses and skyscrapers, temples, churches and mosques. They have made roads and railways to improve communications, and bridges and tunnels to get over or under obstacles. And they have constructed dams to store water or to generate electricity.

The branch of engineering that deals with the construction of massive structures such as skyscrapers, dams and bridges is called civil engineering.

► Civil engineers use giant excavators like this dragline to remove soil from construction sites. They need to dig deep into the ground to prepare foundations for massive structures like dams.

▼ Engineers surveying a construction site. They are levelling, or measuring heights. The engineer on the left is using an electronic theodolite and range-finder to measure the distance and angle to a calibrated staff held by the other engineer.

Once a site has been surveyed, the engineers have to come up with a design for the structure on the site. They also need to choose materials that give their structure the necessary strength. And they prepare detailed engineering drawings of the whole structure and its separate parts, showing how they will fit together.

Site work

For all kinds of construction work, civil engineers have to begin in a similar way. For example, they have to measure (survey) the land accurately so that construction can start in the right place. Surveyors use instruments like theodolites, levels and range-finders.

Theodolites measure angles accurately, using a small telescope that swivels round on a tripod. Levels help surveyors measure the height of the ground. Range-finders measure distances: modern ones work by reflecting laser beams.

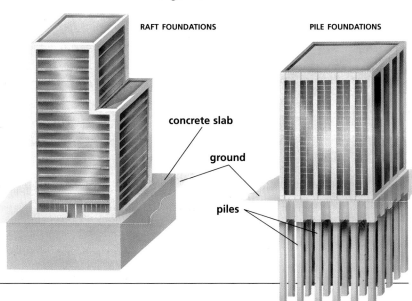

RAFT FOUNDATIONS

PILE FOUNDATIONS

concrete slab

ground

piles

Shifting the muck

When plans have been finalized, work can begin on site. The first task is usually earth-moving (often called muck-shifting). To shift the earth, they use all kinds of machines, including bulldozers, excavators and scrapers.

A bulldozer has a tough, curved blade in front, which can strip off a layer of soil or uproot tree stumps or rocks. It runs on caterpillar tracks so that it can travel better over rough ground. Excavators usually have digging buckets on hydraulic-powered arms, but some are draglines – machines like cranes, that scoop up soil in a large bucket.

Scrapers scoop up soil in a huge bowl with a cutting blade at the bottom. They are used particularly in road-building.

Firm foundations

After the site has been cleared, construction can begin. The first stage is to build a strong supporting base for the structure – the foundations. The bigger the structure, the more massive its foundations will need to be to carry its weight and stop it sinking into the ground.

The best foundations of all are solid rock. There is solid rock just below the surface in New York City, which makes it easy to build skyscrapers there. In most places, however, rock lies too far underground to reach. Then other kinds of foundations must be used.

Rafts and piles

The type and size of the foundations chosen depends on the properties of the soil. As a result of soil tests, engineers may use a raft foundation. This is a huge slab of concrete, which spreads the weight of a structure over a large area. Or they may use pile foundations. Piles are long columns sunk deep into the ground to where there is firm soil.

Sometimes, particularly in bridge construction, foundations have to be built in water. A temporary dam may be built around the site and the water pumped out while the foundations are built. Or, a prefabricated (ready-built) unit called a caisson may be sunk to form the foundations.

◄ Pouring concrete for dam foundations. Concrete is a cheap material for construction and sets as hard as rock. It is strong under compression (squeezing), but weak under tension (stretching). To make it stronger, it is reinforced (strengthened) with steel rods, which are strong under tension.

key words

- civil engineering
- foundations
- piles
- surveying

▼ Four common kinds of foundations, used to provide a firm support for structures. Large buildings may have raft or pile foundations. Houses use concrete 'footings' and blocks. Ready-built concrete caissons are often used to support bridge piers.

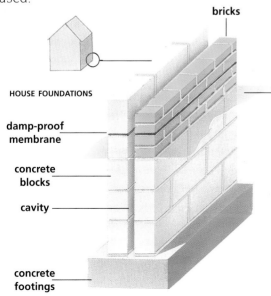

HOUSE FOUNDATIONS

bricks

ground

damp-proof membrane

concrete blocks

cavity

concrete footings

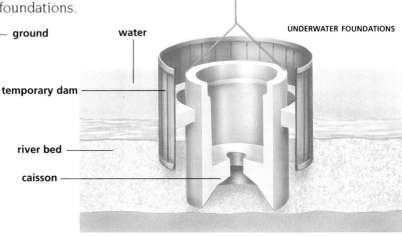

UNDERWATER FOUNDATIONS

water

temporary dam

river bed

caisson

FROM HOMES TO DOMES

In the year 2000, the city of Kuala Lumpur in Malaysia boasted the world's tallest building – the Petronas Towers, which are 452 metres high. But work had already started on buildings that would be even taller. One was 7 South Dearborn in Chicago, USA. When it is completed in 2004, 7 South Dearborn will soar to 472 metres and become in its turn the world's tallest building, but probably not for long.

Very tall buildings like the Petronas Towers are called skyscrapers. The world's first skyscraper, the 10-storey Home Insurance Co. Building, was built in Chicago in 1885.

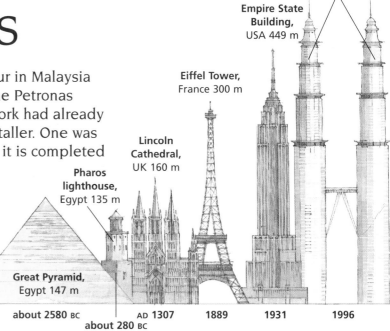

Petronas Towers, Malaysia 452 m

Empire State Building, USA 449 m

Eiffel Tower, France 300 m

Lincoln Cathedral, UK 160 m

Pharos lighthouse, Egypt 135 m

Great Pyramid, Egypt 147 m

about 2580 BC   about 280 BC   AD 1307   1889   1931   1996

Strong to the core

Skyscrapers and most large modern buildings are built with a skeleton of steel girders. Steel is immensely strong, and this is what makes it possible for buildings to soar to such dizzy heights. Many have a central core of reinforced concrete. The floors are built out from the core to an outer steel skeleton.

In these structures, the frame carries all the weight. This means that the walls can be built of thin and lightweight materials. The favourite material for walls is glass, which is fixed in an aluminium or stainless-steel frame. The glass is often covered with a very thin film of gold. This filters out sunlight, and prevents the building heating up like a greenhouse.

Building high

Some tall buildings are built to show off the wealth and importance of a company or city. Others are built for the very good reason that land in cities is scarce and expensive. It is cheaper to expand upwards rather than sideways.

Back home

When you build skyscrapers and tower blocks, the walls are built last. But the walls

▼ Immensely strong steel girders form the framework of this skyscraper, which towers above other city buildings.

▲ Milestones in building construction over the ages, beginning with Egypt's Great Pyramid, completed in about 2580 BC. Like the Pharos lighthouse and Lincoln Cathedral, it was built of stone, unlike modern structures, which are built of steel and concrete.

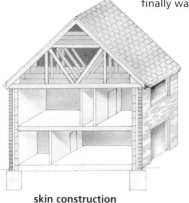

frame construction
steel frame is built
first, then floors and
finally walls

skin construction
skin (outer walls) built first to
support floors and roof

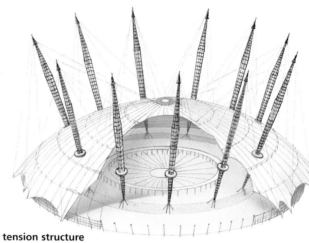

tension structure
steel masts and cables
provide support for
fabric roof

BUILDING WITH MUD

People who lived in what is now Palestine were building mud-brick houses 8000 years ago. And mud bricks, often called adobe, are still used today in countries with a hot, dry climate. They are made from mud and chopped straw, which helps strengthen them. Another traditional mud-building method, called wattle and daub, is used to fill in the spaces in timber-framed buildings. Mud (daub) is applied to a lattice of wooden sticks (wattle).

of an ordinary house are built first because they carry all the weight of the building.

Bricks have been a common material for walling for thousands of years. Early bricks were made of mud and dried in the sun. Modern bricks are made of a clay mixture, and baked in a high-temperature kiln (oven). They are bonded together with a cement mortar.

Many buildings are built with timber frames. Such buildings may be built up of standard sections, which are made elsewhere and then just put together on site. This prefabricated (ready-built) method greatly speeds up construction.

Tension structures

Some of the most exciting buildings being built today are known as tension structures. They include the Hajj airport terminal in Saudi Arabia and London's Millennium Dome. They have tent-like roofs, supported by steel cables in tension. The roofing material is a strong and long-lasting plastic composite.

Domes are a common method of covering large areas, such as sports stadiums. Usually they are supported around the edge. The Pontiac Silverdome Stadium in Detroit, however, has a dome that has no visible means of support, either from below or above. Its fibreglass roof is supported by air pressure. Spectators enter the building through an airlock.

▲ Three quite different methods of building. Ordinary houses are built with outer supporting walls. Tower blocks and skyscrapers have a metal frame to support their weight. Tension structures are an exciting new way of building. They have tent-like roofs supported by cables.

 key words
- brick
- cement
- reinforced concrete
- skyscraper

BRIDGING THE GAP

When the bridge across the Great Belt in Denmark was finished early in 1998, it had the world's longest span – 1624 metres. But before it was officially opened in June, it had lost the record to the Akashi-Kaikyo bridge in Japan, which had a span of 1990 metres.

Both the Great Belt and the Akashi-Kaikyo bridges are suspension bridges. They are spectacular structures, in which the road deck hangs from a pair of steel cables. These cables pass over tall towers and are attached to anchor points at each end.

Like all big bridges, the Akashi-Kaikyo bridge is designed not only to take the weight of heavy traffic, but also to allow for the stresses created by wind. Designers worked out these stresses by testing scale models of the bridge in wind tunnels. They also gave the bridge added strength to help it resist earthquakes.

Beams and arches

There are many other kinds of bridge. The simplest and oldest kind is the beam bridge, which is made out of a beam supported at each end. Beams tend to sag in the middle, so simple beam bridges cannot cross a very wide gap.

▶ Different kinds of bridges can span different widths. Suspension bridges can be built with the longest spans. Cable-stayed bridges are now widely built.

beam bridge

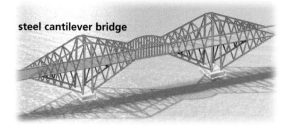

steel cantilever bridge

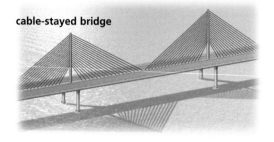

cable-stayed bridge

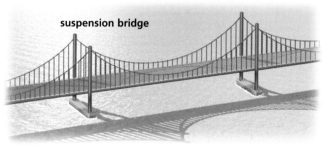

suspension bridge

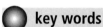
key words

- arch
- deck
- foundations
- span
- wind tunnel

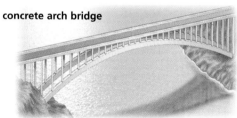

concrete arch bridge

A long beam bridge can be built if the beam is supported by piers (columns). Even longer spans can be built by using cables to stiffen the deck. This produces what is called a cable-stayed bridge, in which cables lead from the deck to a tall central tower.

Arch bridges can be used for wide spans too, because the weight of the bridge is carried down to the foundations by the arch shape.

◀ The steel-arch Sydney Harbour Bridge (1932) has a central span of 503 metres. The deck carries eight traffic lanes and a railway.

BUILDING ROADS

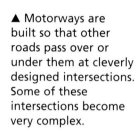

There is a road that starts in north-west Alaska and runs south through North America, into Central America and on into South America. It then heads east and finally ends in Brasília, the capital of Brazil. It is the Pan-American Highway, which stretches for an astonishing 24,140 kilometres.

Every year more than 50 million new vehicles – cars, vans, trucks and buses – flood on to the world's roads, adding to the hundreds of millions already there. Road systems are continually being improved. Old roads are widened and new ones built.

Under construction

Before people start to build a road they have to decide on a suitable route. This often needs to be agreed with local government, local people and environmental groups.

Once agreement is reached, the route can be cleared and levelled. The next step is to build the bridges, tunnels and junctions.

Most roads are paved with a mixture of crushed stone and tar, called tarmac or asphalt. The road has a rounded top surface, or camber, to allow rainwater to run off. Drains along the edge carry the water away.

Motorways

Motorways are a type of road specially designed to handle large volumes of high-speed traffic. They have no traffic lights, roundabouts or junctions – drivers can only stop on a motorway if their vehicle breaks down. Motorways are built as level and as straight as possible so that traffic does not have to slow down for corners or hills.

▲ Motorways are built so that other roads pass over or under them at cleverly designed intersections. Some of these intersections become very complex.

key words
- camber
- intersection
- motorway

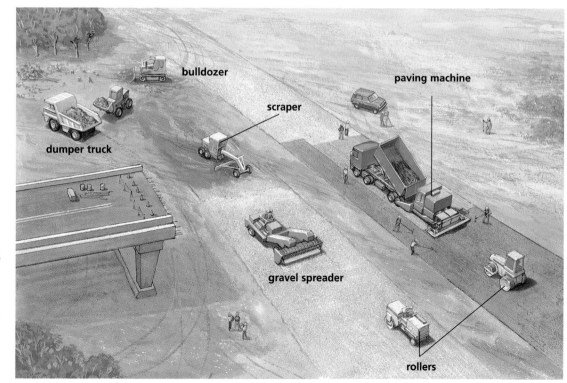

▶ Road-building uses many machines to prepare the ground and lay the surface. Bulldozers and scrapers clear the ground; dumper trucks remove soil and bring in crushed stone for the foundations and tarmac for the surface. Paving machines spread the tarmac, while rollers compact it and roll it flat.

bulldozer

scraper

paving machine

dumper truck

gravel spreader

rollers

STOPPING THE FLOW

The year is 2010. After more than 15 years' work, the Three Gorges dam on the River Yangtze in China is finished. At last the mighty Yangtze – whose floods killed 300,000 people in the 20th century – has been tamed.

Engineers build dams to stop flooding, store water and improve navigation. The water stored behind a dam is called a reservoir. This water is often used as a source of power. It is fed through water turbines that spin generators to produce electricity. This is hydroelectric power.

Sheer weight

Dams are the biggest of all man-made structures. The Three Gorges dam, for example, will be massive – about 2 kilometres long and 175 metres high and containing 30 million cubic metres of concrete.

Three Gorges is a type of dam known as a gravity dam. Its huge weight keeps it in place and holds back the water behind it. Even larger gravity dams are built using soil, rock and clay. They are called earth-fill or embankment dams. The biggest, such as the Syncrude Tailings dam in Alberta, Canada, contain more than 500 million cubic metres of earth-fill.

Some dams have a different design. They are made of concrete, but it is their shape not their weight that gives them strength. They have a curved, arch shape, with the outward curve facing upstream. The curving concrete carries the water pressure to firm foundations at the sides and base.

Affecting the environment

Dams bring a lot of benefits, but they can also bring problems to communities and the environment. The reservoir created by the Three Gorges dam will submerge more than 150 towns, and make up to 1,500,000 people homeless. Dams also reduce the flow of water down a river, which can have environmental effects.

▶ The embankment dam is made up of earth and rock. It has a clay core to make it watertight. The concrete gravity dam has a triangular cross-section. The arch dam is slender, but its shape makes it strong. The columns of the buttress dam give it extra strength.

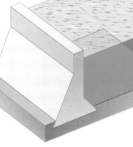

CONCRETE GRAVITY DAM

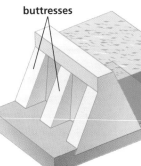

buttresses

BUTTRESS DAM

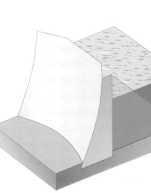

CONCRETE ARCH DAM

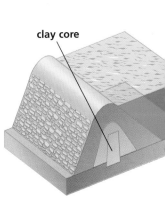

clay core

EMBANKMENT DAM

◀ The Hoover Dam on the Colorado River, USA. Completed in 1936, it is a huge concrete-arch dam, 221 metres high. The enormous reservoir behind the dam is called Lake Mead.

key words

- arch
- earth-fill
- gravity
- hydroelectric

TUNNELS AND PIPES

At 11.13 am precisely on 1 December 1990, Britain ceased to be an island. At that moment, a tunnel dug from England towards France broke through into one dug from France towards England under the English Channel. Amazingly, the tunnels were only 50 centimetres out of line. This tunnel was to form part of the Channel Tunnel.

Like all the biggest transport tunnels, the Channel Tunnel is a rail tunnel. It is 50 kilometres long – only 4 kilometres shorter than the longest rail tunnel in the world, the Seikan Tunnel in Japan, which also goes under the sea. Road tunnels tend to be much shorter. The St Gotthard tunnel through the Alps is the longest, at 16 kilometres.

▶ The Trans-Alaskan Pipeline carries oil from wells in the north of Alaska. It is 1285 kilometres long. About half of the pipeline is carried above ground, half is underground.

Boring tunnels

You can dig shallow tunnels by digging a deep ditch and then covering it over to form a tunnel. This is called cut-and-cover. Underground railways are sometimes built this way. But if you are digging a deep tunnel you must use other methods, depending on the nature of the ground.

When you are drilling through hard rock, you use explosives to break up the rock face. The explosives are placed inside holes drilled by a 'jumbo' drilling rig. Then they are detonated (set off).

When drilling through softer rock, such as chalk, you use huge tunnel-boring machines (TBMs). TBMs are also used for tunnelling through soft or wet ground. Then they are fitted with a pressurized cutting head. The air pressure helps stop the tunnel caving in before the tunnel segments are put in place.

▼ A TBM has a rotating cutting head at the front, studded with sharp teeth. As the TBM moves forwards, ring-shaped segments are put in place to form the tunnel wall.

key words

- Channel Tunnel
- cut-and-cover
- explosives
- TBM

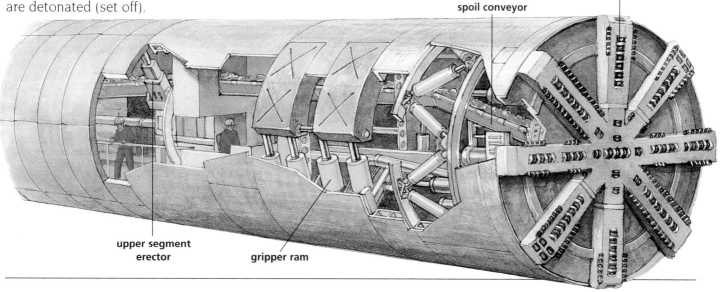

cutterhead

spoil conveyor

upper segment erector

gripper ram

ON THE MOVE

In 1492, it took Christopher Columbus more than a month to sail across the Atlantic Ocean to the 'New World' (America). Today, a supersonic aircraft can make the journey in less then three hours, travelling faster than a rifle bullet.

Two hundred years ago, most people did not travel far from their homes. But with the invention of engines to power first ships and trains, then later cars and planes, travelling became easier, quicker and cheaper. Indeed, today there are so many people travelling that transport systems throughout the world are becoming congested (clogged up).

On land

On land, motor vehicles are quick and convenient, but there are so many of them that they are beginning to jam our roads, especially in cities. Even worse, their exhaust fumes cause dangerous pollution that threatens our health and the environment. Electrically-powered and even solar-powered vehicles could be the way ahead, because they cause hardly any pollution.

Railways are less important than they used to be because of competition from other vehicles. But they remain one of the most energy-efficient forms of transport. They can haul heavy loads at high speed, and they cause little pollution. As traffic jams on the roads increase, trains are becoming more popular.

By air and sea

For really long journeys, most people travel by plane. At peak times, airports are filled to overflowing. The planned new 'Super Jumbo' jets carrying over 600 passengers will make the airports busier still.

200 YEARS OF TRANSPORT

ROAD TRANSPORT

1885
Karl Benz (Germany) builds the first motor car, a three-wheeled vehicle powered by a petrol engine.

RAIL TRANSPORT

1804
Richard Trevithick (Britain) builds the first successful steam locomotive, for the Pen-y-Darren tramway in Wales.

SEA TRANSPORT

1807
The US engineer Robert Fulton designs the *Clermont*, the first successful steamboat.

AIR TRANSPORT

1783
The French Montgolfier brothers, Joseph-Michel and Jacques-Étienne, make the first flight in a hot-air balloon in Paris.

1885
Englishman John Starley makes the first Rover Safety Cycle, with all the features of a modern bicycle.

1830
George Stephenson (Britain) builds the first passenger railway, the Liverpool and Manchester Railway. He and his son Robert design a new locomotive to run on it, the 'Rocket'.

1838
First voyage of Isambard Kingdom Brunel's (Britain) SS *Great Western*, the first steamship to make regular Atlantic crossings.

1804
Sir George Cayley (Britain) builds the first heavier-than-air flying machine, a glider.

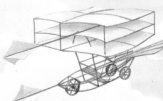

Ships are the best way to transport heavy loads over very long distances. The biggest ships are oil tankers. They can be half a kilometre long, and they take several kilometres to stop. Short sea crossings are being speeded up by ferries like the Sea Cat. This is a catamaran (a ship with two hulls) that can cruise at speeds of about 70 kilometres per hour.

 key words
- catamaran
- congestion
- supersonic aircraft
- traffic

1908
Henry Ford (USA) introduces the Model T, the first car to be produced cheaply and in really large numbers.

1937
Volkswagen ('people's car') launched in Germany: later nicknamed the Beetle.

1990s
'People carriers' like the Renault Espace become popular.

1997
Thrust SSC (Britain) breaks the sound barrier with a new world land speed record of 1228 km/h.

1912
The first diesel locomotive runs in Germany.

1938
The streamlined *Mallard* (Britain) sets the all-time speed record for steam.

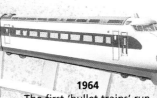

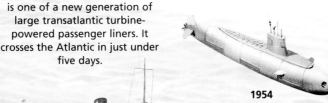

1964
The first 'bullet trains' run on Japan's Shinkansen high-speed railway.

1990
A TGV (Train à Grande Vitesse) travels at the record speed of over 515 km/h.

1894
Charles Parsons (Britain) demonstrates the first boat powered by steam turbines, *Turbinia*.

1907
The *Mauretania* (Britain) is one of a new generation of large transatlantic turbine-powered passenger liners. It crosses the Atlantic in just under five days.

1954
The first nuclear-powered submarine, *Nautilus* (USA), is launched.

1959
Christopher Cockerell (Britain) designs the first hovercraft.

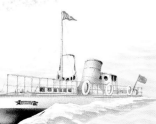

1947
Charles Yeager (USA) breaks the sound barrier in a Bell X-1 rocket plane.

1900
Ferdinand Graf von Zeppelin (Germany) builds the first large rigid airship, 128 m long.

1903
The Wright Brothers (USA) build and fly the first powered aeroplane, *Flyer I*, at Kitty Hawk, North Carolina.

1939
The first jet aircraft flies, the Heinkel He 178 (Germany). Igor Sikorsky (Russia) establishes the design of the single-rotor helicopter.

1969
The Boeing 747 jumbo jet (USA) and the supersonic airliner Concorde (England, France) make their first flights.

BIKES AND MOTORBIKES

With a strong, light frame, chunky tyres, good suspension and up to 24 gears, a mountain bike is designed for off-road use. It lets you go where you want – along muddy tracks, down rocky slopes, through streams and over potholes.

Mountain bikes are specially built for rough riding. The frames are built more strongly than road bike frames, they have better brakes, and extra-low gears for getting up really steep slopes. But they are heavier than road bikes, and the chunky tyres make them harder work on smooth roads.

Bicycle basics

All bicycles work in much the same way. They have a strong, light frame and spoked wheels, fitted with air-filled tyres. They are driven by a chain, which connects the pedals with the rear wheel.

Bicycle frames are most commonly made from steel, or an alloy (mixture) of steel and a lighter metal. But expensive bikes have super-light frames made of aluminium, titanium, or plastic reinforced with carbon fibre.

Most bicycles have several gears. The commonest kind are called derailleur gears. They have different-sized gear wheels attached to the pedals and on the rear wheel. A mechanism shifts the chain from one gear wheel to another.

Under power

Motorcycles are a cross between a bicycle and a motor car. Like a bicycle, they are steered by the front wheel, and most have the rear wheel driven by a chain. Like a car, they have a petrol engine, a clutch and a gearbox. Some motorbikes have a shaft instead of a chain connecting the engine to the rear wheel.

Motorcycles have similar kinds of brakes to a car. They work by hydraulic (liquid) pressure. Applying the brakes forces tough pads to grip a disc mounted on the wheel.

▲ Motorbikes are used for fun as well as for transport. These jumping motorbikes are competing in a moto-cross race.

 key words

- alloy
- derailleur
- gears
- hydraulic

▼ Bicycle technology has improved enormously in recent years. New frame materials, brake designs, and front and rear suspension are just some of the changes that have been introduced.

one-click levers quickly move the gear mechanism from one gear wheel to the next

lightweight wheels are made of aluminium alloy or carbon fibre. They may have a few large spokes, or even be solid

cantilever brakes pivot as the lever is pulled, to press the brake blocks against the wheel

new frame designs are possible using materials such as carbon-fibre plastics

suspension at front and rear smooths the ride over rough ground

CARS AND TRUCKS

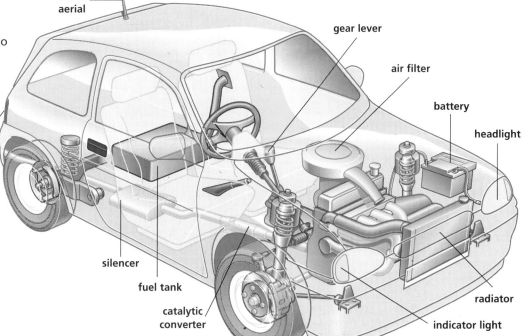

A hundred years ago, the streets of most cities were filled with the clattering of hooves, the creak of wooden wheels, and the smells of manure. But within 50 years, carts pulled by animals had been replaced by the 'horseless carriage' – the car.

Today, hundreds of millions of motor vehicles run on the world's roads, and up to 50 million new ones are made each year. Most of these vehicles are cars. The rest are commercial vehicles such as trucks and buses. In richer countries especially, the car plays an important part in people's lives. It influences where they live and work, and what they do in their leisure time.

Health warning

Cars are not all good news – they can be dangerous. Tens of thousands of people around the world are killed each year in car accidents. Cars also emit (give off) carbon dioxide gas and other fumes that pollute the air. Some of these fumes are bad for people's health. Others are part of the cause of the greenhouse effect, which is gradually warming our climate.

The outer shell

The body of most vehicles is made from steel sheets, welded together. Cars usually have an all-in-one body shell. Design engineers test model vehicles in wind tunnels, to make the shape as streamlined as possible.

Rather than an all-in-one body, most commercial vehicles have a strong frame, or chassis, separate from the body.

The engine

Two main kinds of engine are used in motor vehicles – petrol and diesel engines. Cars most commonly have petrol engines, while most commercial vehicles have diesel engines. Motor manufacturers normally fit devices called catalytic converters to reduce the harmful fumes these engines emit. They are also testing

▲ A Formula 1 racing car is fitted with aerofoils, or wings, front and back. As they move through the air, they produce a downwards force that makes the car hold the road better.

key words
- brakes
- cooling system
- engine
- exhaust
- pollution
- steering
- suspension
- transmission

▶ A car is made up of a number of systems, which link together to make it work. They include the body, the engine, transmission, brakes, the steering system, the suspension system and the electrical system.

KEY
- engine
- transmission
- gearbox
- cooling system
- exhaust
- steering
- brakes
- electrical system
- suspension

radio aerial

gear lever

air filter

battery

headlight

tail light

exhaust pipe

silencer

fuel tank

catalytic converter

radiator

indicator light

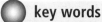

engines that run on liquefied petroleum gas (LPG) and electric cars powered by new batteries called fuel cells. These cause less pollution.

The transmission

The transmission system transmits power from the engine to the wheels. The major parts are the clutch and the gearbox.

If you want to ride a bicycle up a steep hill, you need a low gear. In a high gear, your legs just aren't strong enough to turn the pedals. Cars and trucks need gears for similar reasons. Some vehicles have a manual gearbox, while others change gear automatically.

The clutch smoothly disconnects and re-connects the engine with the rest of the transmission as a driver changes gear. Without the clutch, the gearbox would be damaged by gear-changes.

In some cars and most trucks, the transmission drives the rear wheels. But most modern cars have an engine at the front driving the front wheels. Some vehicles have four-wheel drive, with the engine driving both pairs of wheels.

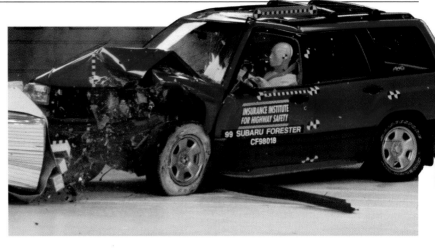

▲ Manufacturers carry out crash tests to make sure that cars are as safe as possible in an accident. Modern car bodies have 'crumple zones' at the front and back, designed to absorb some of the impact of a crash.

The brakes

Brakes are designed to slow down a vehicle quickly and safely. Heavy trucks and buses have powerful air brakes, which work using compressed air. Cars have hydraulic brakes, which work by liquid pressure. When the driver presses the brake pedal, pipes full of brake fluid (liquid) carry the pressure to the wheels. At each wheel, the liquid pushes on a piston, which presses the brake pads against a disc or drum on the wheel.

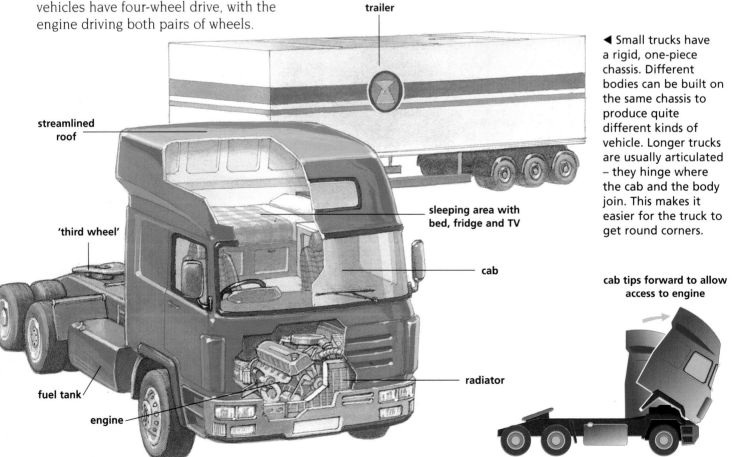

trailer

streamlined roof

'third wheel'

fuel tank

engine

sleeping area with bed, fridge and TV

cab

radiator

◀ Small trucks have a rigid, one-piece chassis. Different bodies can be built on the same chassis to produce quite different kinds of vehicle. Longer trucks are usually articulated – they hinge where the cab and the body join. This makes it easier for the truck to get round corners.

cab tips forward to allow access to engine

ON THE RAILS

When the Italian high-speed train, 'Il Pendolino', comes to a bend, it doesn't slow down. It 'leans into the bend', just as you lean into a corner on your bike. By tilting, the train can corner faster.

Tilting trains are a way of running faster trains on existing railway tracks. But in several countries, specially designed straight railway tracks have been built for new high-speed trains.

Japan began the high-speed train revolution in 1964 with the Shinkansen (the New Trunk Line). Today, France has the fastest trains, the TGVs (Trains à Grande Vitesse). They regularly reach speeds of up to 260 kilometres per hour.

▲ A few steam trains still run in India on track with a narrower width (gauge) than usual. Narrow-gauge railways also run in other countries, often on a 1-metre gauge.

key words
- gauge
- locomotive
- maglev
- rapid transit

▼ Locomotives are electric, diesel or steam-powered. Only a few steam locomotives remain, most of them run by rail enthusiasts.

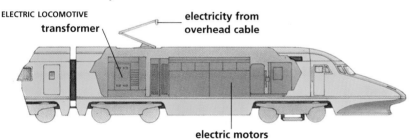

ELECTRIC LOCOMOTIVE
transformer — electricity from overhead cable — electric motors

DIESEL LOCOMOTIVE — cooling fans — generator powered by diesel — electric motors — diesel engine — steam powers piston

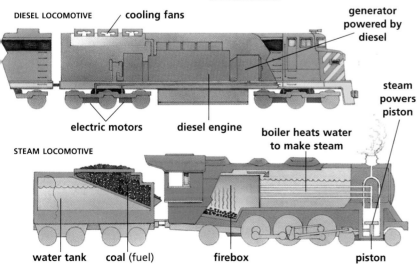

STEAM LOCOMOTIVE — boiler heats water to make steam — water tank — coal (fuel) — firebox — piston

The track
Trains run on steel wheels on a steel track. This is a very efficient arrangement. The wheels have flanges (rims) on the inside to keep them on the track. The steel track is laid on wooden or concrete cross-pieces called sleepers.

In most countries, the two rails of the track are 143.5 cm apart, known as the standard gauge. This is the width of track George Stephenson chose when he built the first railways in England in the 1830s. Other gauges are used in some countries.

Not all railway tracks have two rails. Some have a single track and are called monorails. In some designs, the train hangs from trolleys that run along the rail. In others, the car straddles the rail. Straddle monorails are used to carry holidaymakers around the Disneyland pleasure parks.

Locomotives
The first railways used steam power to haul wagons and carriages. Steam locomotives were heavy machines that used fuel

inefficiently and were very dirty. A few steam locomotives are still in use, but in most countries they have been replaced by diesels or electric locomotives.

Diesel locomotives have diesel engines, which burn oil as fuel. Most are diesel-electric units. This means that they use their engines to drive electricity generators. The electricity produced powers electric motors, which turn the locomotive wheels.

Electric locomotives pick up the electricity to power their electric motors from an outside source. Usually this is an overhead power line. The lines operate at very high voltage.

In some countries, notably Britain, some electric lines are worked from a third rail. The locomotives pick up electricity from a live rail that runs alongside the ordinary track. The trains on London's Underground operate on a third-rail system.

Going underground

There are underground railways in more than 100 cities around the world. They are known by such names as the subway, the metro, the rapid-transit system or mass-transit system. The London Underground is the world's largest underground railway, with more than 400 kilometres of track. It does not stay underground for all its

FLYING TRAINS

A French TGV has travelled at a speed of more than 515 kilometres per hour. This is close to the maximum speed that a train with wheels can travel without slipping. To travel faster, railway engineers are experimenting with trains without wheels that float above the track, using magnetism. This type of train is called a maglev, short for magnetic levitation.

▼ A heavily loaded freight train pulls its cargo through the Rocky Mountains in the USA. Often such freight trains have two or even three locomotives, to give them enough power to haul their huge loads.

length, but runs on the surface and high-level tracks as well.

Cities are building or expanding their underground railway networks to help reduce traffic congestion on the surface.

ON THE WING

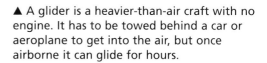

Just after dawn on 21 March 1999, a silvery balloon as tall as a skyscraper landed in the sand of the Egyptian desert. *Breitling Orbiter 3* had set off from a snowy village in Switzerland 19 days earlier. Its crew, Bertrand Piccard (Switzerland) and Brian Jones (Britain), had become the first people to fly around the world by balloon.

The first aircraft to lift a human into the skies was a balloon. But it is heavier-than-air craft such as aeroplanes and helicopters that dominate our skies today. Almost every minute of every day, airliners carrying up to 400 people take off from or land at our main airports.

Lighter than air

Balloons fly because they are light: they float in air in the same way that boats float in water. There are two main types – hot-air balloons and gas balloons. Hot-air balloons are filled with air heated by a burner. Because the hot air is lighter (less dense) than the surrounding cold air, the balloon floats upwards. Gas balloons are filled with a light gas, usually helium.

▼ *Breitling Orbiter 3* on its way to becoming the first balloon to fly non-stop around the world. Unlike most balloons, the *Breitling Orbiter* used a combination of helium gas and hot air. Climbing as high as 11,755 metres above the Earth's surface, the crew travelled in a sealed capsule with its own air supply.

▲ A glider is a heavier-than-air craft with no engine. It has to be towed behind a car or aeroplane to get into the air, but once airborne it can glide for hours.

Airships are elongated balloons, fitted with engines. In the early 20th century, huge airships pioneered long-distance air travel. Today, small airships are used for such things as aerial photography.

Heavier than air

How can something as big and as heavy as a 400-tonne airliner leave the ground and stay in the air? The answer lies in the wings. A wing has a special shaped cross-section, called an aerofoil. When air flows across the wing, it tends to lift upwards. It is this lifting force that supports the plane in the air. Like birds, planes need a tail as well as wings. The tail helps to keep the plane steady. It has a vertical tail fin and horizontal tailplanes.

Building aircraft

Most aircraft are made out of lightweight materials, particularly aluminium alloys. These are nearly as strong as steel but much lighter. For key parts of the aircraft, especially those that get hot, titanium or stainless steel may be used. These metals stay strong even at high temperatures.

The main structure of a plane (the airframe) is made up of a framework of ribs and spars. On top is a thin shell of aluminium sheets. In parts where extra strength is required, such as the wings, the airframe may be made out of a single piece of metal.

The jet set

An aeroplane's engines provide the power, or thrust, to move it along. Until the 1950s, most planes were powered by piston engines, which turned large propellers. But most planes now have jet engines.

A jet engine burns fuel to produce a jet of high-speed gases. As the jet shoots backwards, it moves the plane forwards. In the turbofan engines used in airliners, the jet of gases also turns a large fan, which pushes large amounts of cooler air out backwards, too. Turboprops are engines which use the jet of gas to spin a propeller.

Keeping in shape

All planes have the same basic parts – wings, fuselage (body), engines and tail – but they vary widely in design. The greatest differences between aircraft lie in the shape of their wings. Slow planes have long wings that stick out from the fuselage almost at right-angles. But higher-speed planes have wings that are swept back at an angle.

The overall shape of a plane is streamlined, so that it slips through the air easily. Aircraft designers test models of their craft in wind tunnels. This gives them a good idea of how the real planes will behave flying through the air.

▲ The eurofighter is one of the world's most advanced fighter planes. It is powered by twin jet engines, and has a sharply pointed nose and delta (triangular) wings for supersonic flight. The body and wings are made not from metal, but from plastics reinforced with carbon fibre.

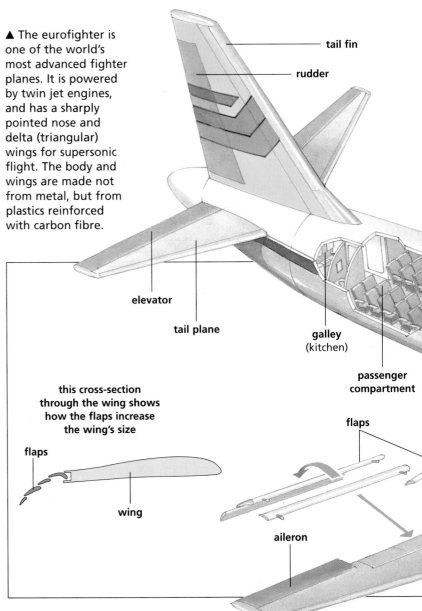

tail fin

rudder

elevator

tail plane

galley (kitchen)

passenger compartment

this cross-section through the wing shows how the flaps increase the wing's size

flaps

flaps

wing

aileron

Vertical take-off

Most aeroplanes need a long runway for taking off and landing. The plane has to be moving quite fast before the wings produce enough lift to get it off the ground. But a few aircraft can take off and land vertically. The Harrier jump-jet is a VTOL (vertical take-off and landing) aeroplane. But the most widely used VTOL craft is the helicopter.

Like an aeroplane, a helicopter is supported in the air by wings. These wings are the blades of the rotor, which spins round on top of the helicopter's body. The rotor blades have the same aerofoil shape as ordinary wings. But instead of the aircraft moving forwards to create lift, the rotor spins round.

▶ A US coastguard helicopter carrying out a rescue on the coast of north California. The rotation of the helicopter's rotor tends to make the body of the helicopter spin. To stop this happening, there is a small rotor at the tail, facing sideways.

key words
- aerofoil
- lift
- rotor
- supersonic
- thrust
- vertical take-off

By 2006, the Airbus A380 (the 'Super-Jumbo') could be flying. Measuring about 79 metres long and about the same across the wings, the A380 will carry more than 600 passengers. Fully loaded, it will weigh nearly 600 tonnes.

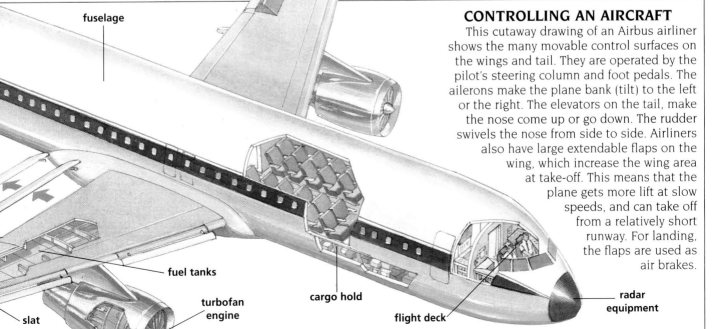

fuselage

spoilers (air brakes)

fuel tanks

turbofan engine

cargo hold

flight deck

slat

radar equipment

CONTROLLING AN AIRCRAFT
This cutaway drawing of an Airbus airliner shows the many movable control surfaces on the wings and tail. They are operated by the pilot's steering column and foot pedals. The ailerons make the plane bank (tilt) to the left or the right. The elevators on the tail, make the nose come up or go down. The rudder swivels the nose from side to side. Airliners also have large extendable flaps on the wing, which increase the wing area at take-off. This means that the plane gets more lift at slow speeds, and can take off from a relatively short runway. For landing, the flaps are used as air brakes.

SAILING THE SEAS

What floats, is as big as an aircraft carrier, carries over 3,000 passengers, and has an ice rink, a rock-climbing wall, a library and street musicians? The answer is the world's biggest cruise liner, *Voyager of the Seas*, which was launched in November 1999.

Cruise liners are now some of the biggest ships being built. The only ships that are bigger are the supertankers that transport oil around the world. They really are huge – nearly 500 metres long, with space for over 500,000 tonnes of oil.

Keeping afloat

How can such huge vessels, weighing many thousand tonnes, float on water? The answer is that an object can float if it displaces (pushes aside) a weight of liquid equal to its own weight. This displaced water creates an upward force, or upthrust, which keeps the object afloat.

Under power

All ships are pushed along by propellers. Most ships use diesel engines to spin the propellers, but a few, including some ice-breakers, submarines and aircraft carriers, are nuclear-powered. In these ships a nuclear reactor is used to heat water in a boiler. The water turns to steam, and jets of steam are then used to turn turbines (large, many-bladed rotors or propellers). The turbines spin the ship's propellers.

Building ships

Ship designers try to make their vessels as streamlined as possible, to reduce water resistance, or drag. Designers test scale models of their craft in water tanks to get an idea of how the real ships will behave.

Most ships are made from strong steel plates welded together on an inner framework. A few ships have hulls made from other materials, such as glass-fibre.

▶ A supertanker arrives at an oil terminal. These huge ships are difficult to manoeuvre in the tight space of a harbour. They have to be pushed up to the jetty by small but powerful tugboats.

 key words

- drag
- hovercraft
- hydrofoil
- propeller
- turbine

The inside of the hull is divided into several watertight compartments. This strengthens the hull and provides a safety feature, because individual compartments can be sealed off if they become flooded.

On water wings

Ordinary ships move quite slowly through the water because of the water resistance on their hulls. Craft known as hydrofoils

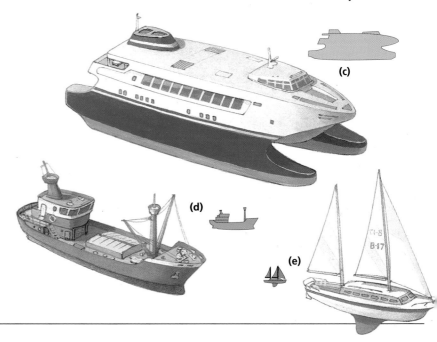

(c)

(d)

(e)

overcome this problem by lifting their hulls right out of the water. A hydrofoil has 'wings', or foils, fitted beneath the hull. When the boat moves forwards, the foils produce a lifting force, just as a plane's wings do in air. The hull lifts clear of the water, and the boat can travel much faster.

Under the waves

Some ships can travel underwater as well as on the surface. Submarines dive underwater or rise to the surface using large ballast tanks, which can be filled with water or air. If the tanks are filled with water, the submarine becomes heavier than the water around it, and sinks. To come up again, air is pumped into the tanks. Air is lighter than water, so the submarine rises to the surface.

Small submarines called submersibles are mostly used for underwater exploration. They are usually powered by electric motors. Large naval submarines are powered by a nuclear reactor. Nuclear submarines can remain submerged for months at a time, but conventional submarines need to surface regularly to recharge their batteries.

▶ This LR5 submersible is a 'lockout' design. It has a sealed diving compartment in which divers can be carried down to the seabed under pressure.

FLOATING ON AIR

Hovercraft glide over the surface on a cushion of air. They can travel at speeds up to about 120 kilometres an hour. A hovercraft looks rather like a huge rubber dinghy, with a 'skirt' around its hull. Powerful fans blow air underneath the craft, and the skirt stops it leaking away too quickly.

engine turns fan and propeller

air drawn in

fan

skirt

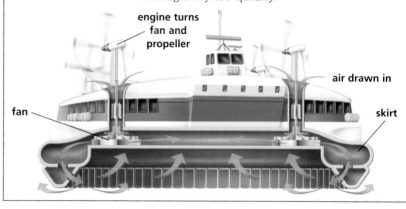

(a)

(b)

◀ Some of the many different types of ship. The small silhouettes with each picture show the relative sizes of each vessel. Container ships (a) are the most common cargo ships. Large passenger ferries (b) are used on the busiest routes. (c) A super-fast trimaran ferry. The trawler (d) is the most common type of fishing vessel. Sailing boats (e) are used mainly for pleasure.

FINDING THE WAY

How do you find your way at night if you don't have a map or a compass? You look up at the stars. If you live north of the Equator, look for the Plough. Two of its stars always point to the Pole Star, which points the way north.

Years ago, people used to find their way around by looking up at the sky. By day they looked at the Sun and by night at the stars. Today, other objects in the sky help us navigate. They are navigation satellites. Most planes and ships now use satellite navigation. It is also available for walkers and for use in cars.

Other systems

Before satellite navigation came into use, ships and planes – and walkers too – relied on other methods, such as maps and compasses. Navigators also had devices such as the sextant, to measure the positions of the Sun and stars.

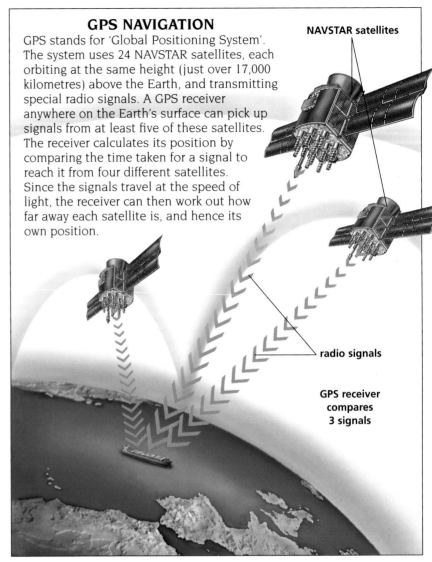

GPS NAVIGATION

GPS stands for 'Global Positioning System'. The system uses 24 NAVSTAR satellites, each orbiting at the same height (just over 17,000 kilometres) above the Earth, and transmitting special radio signals. A GPS receiver anywhere on the Earth's surface can pick up signals from at least five of these satellites. The receiver calculates its position by comparing the time taken for a signal to reach it from four different satellites. Since the signals travel at the speed of light, the receiver can then work out how far away each satellite is, and hence its own position.

NAVSTAR satellites

radio signals

GPS receiver compares 3 signals

◀ This in-car navigation system does not show the car's position. However, it can show detailed route maps and give up-to-date information on local traffic hold-ups.

key words

- compass
- GPS
- inertial navigation
- latitude
- longitude
- satellite

Inertial navigation systems are used in planes, ships, submarines, missiles and spacecraft. These systems provide a constant check on a vehicle's position by sensing every change in speed and direction it makes.

Latitude and longitude

The position of any object on the Earth's surface is pinpointed by its latitude and longitude. The latitude tells you how many degrees the object is north or south of the Equator. Longitude is how many degrees the object is east or west of a line through Greenwich, England.

In atlases, the maps have grid lines on them. These are lines of latitude (running from left to right) and longitude (running from top to bottom).

SEEING WITH ECHOES

A round a busy airport, the skies are full of planes. Some have just taken off. Others are coming in to land. Some are 'stacked up', circling and waiting to land. Yet air-traffic controllers know exactly where each plane is, and can make sure that there are no collisions, thanks to radar.

Radar detects objects by bouncing radio beams off them. It uses very short radio waves called microwaves, which can 'see' through clouds and in the dark.

Radar has many uses besides air traffic control. Ships use radar to avoid collisions at night or in bad weather. Astronomers use radar to map the surface of planets, and police use hand-held radar 'guns' to check the speed of motorists. Rain reflects radar beams, so weather scientists and aircraft can use radar to spot storms.

In a radar system, a rotating aerial sends out narrow beams of microwaves. When a beam hits an object (a plane, say) it is reflected back as a kind of echo. The longer the echo takes to return, the further away the plane is. On the radar screen, a bright spot shows the position of the plane. A signal picked up by another aerial from the plane's own radar gives the plane's identification number and height.

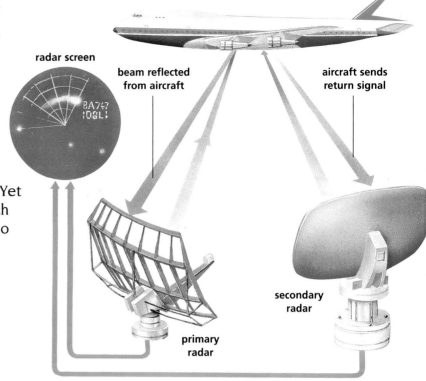

radar screen

beam reflected from aircraft

aircraft sends return signal

secondary radar

primary radar

▲ Two kinds of radar system operate at airports. *Primary radar* finds the position of an aircraft by sending out a radar beam and detecting the echo as it reflects back from the plane.

Secondary radar sends out a beam to a special device on the aircraft. This sends back a signal giving the plane's height and identification number.

Seeing with sound

Radar signals cannot travel through water, so ships and submarines use a kind of 'sound radar', called sonar, to measure depth and to detect things in the water.

The sound waves used are ultrasonic, which means that they are too high-pitched for the ear to detect. Hospitals use ultrasound scanners to produce sound 'pictures' of a baby still inside its mother.

key words

- echo
- microwaves
- navigation
- scan
- ultrasonic

◄ The Air Traffic Control Centre at San Francisco International Airport. The round green radar screens show the position of aircraft flying within about 80 kilometres of the airport.

ARTIFICIAL MOONS

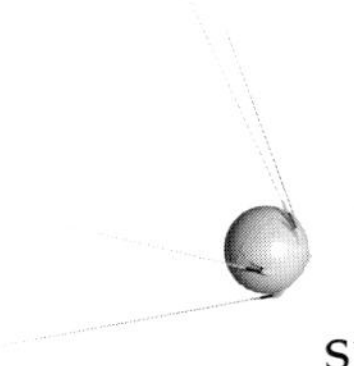

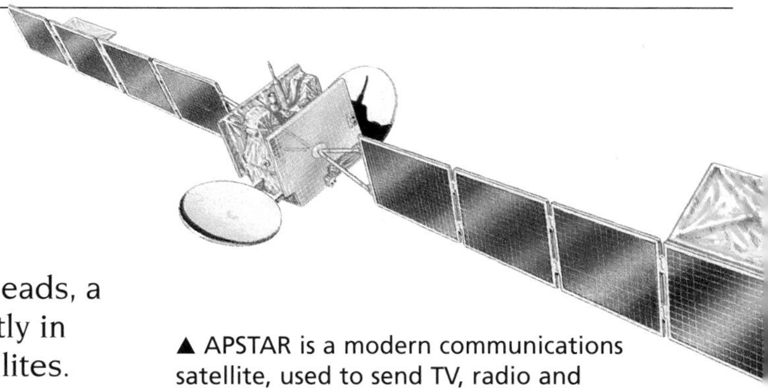

Hundreds of kilometres above our heads, a swarm of tiny 'moons' travels silently in space. They are artificial moons, or satellites. They circle endlessly around the Earth in a constant path, or orbit.

▲ APSTAR is a modern communications satellite, used to send TV, radio and telephone signals around the world.

Up in space, satellites do many things to help us down on Earth. Communications satellites relay (pass on) all kinds of communications signals. These signals include TV programmes, telephone calls and e-mail messages. Weather satellites take pictures of clouds and measure conditions in the air.

Remote-sensing satellites take pictures of the Earth's surface in light of different colours. These pictures show up details that cannot be seen in ordinary photographs. Astronomy satellites carry telescopes into space, where they can see more clearly. Navigation satellites help ships to travel across the oceans and aircraft to find their way in the sky. They are even used by walkers in wild places.

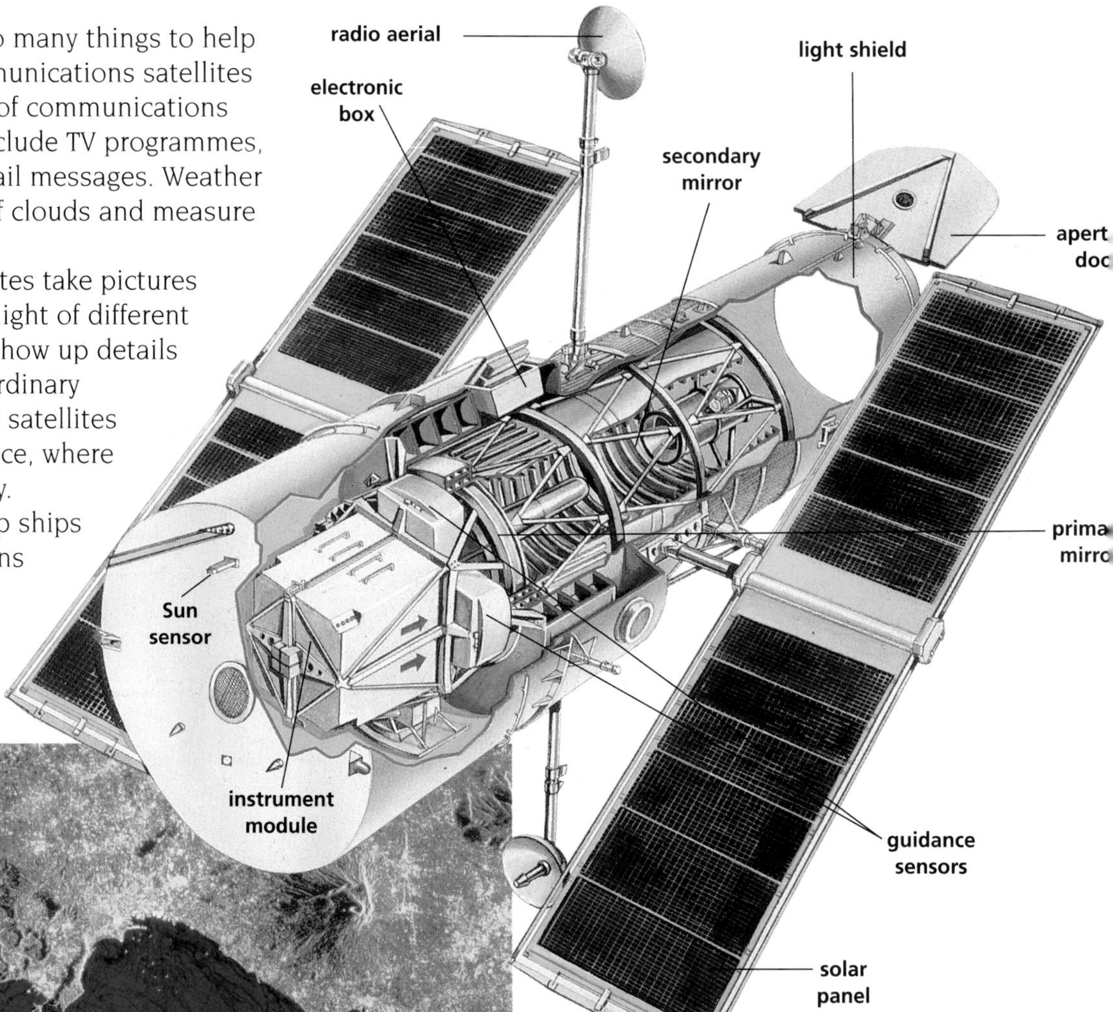

radio aerial

electronic box

light shield

secondary mirror

apert doc

Sun sensor

prima mirro

instrument module

guidance sensors

solar panel

▲ In the Hubble Space Telescope, light is collected by a curved primary mirror 2.4 metres across. Images (pictures) are produced inside the instrument module. The pictures are sent back to Earth as radio signals.

◄ The European remote-sensing satellite ERS-1 sent back this picture of the Bay of Naples in Italy. The colours in the image are false – not true to life.

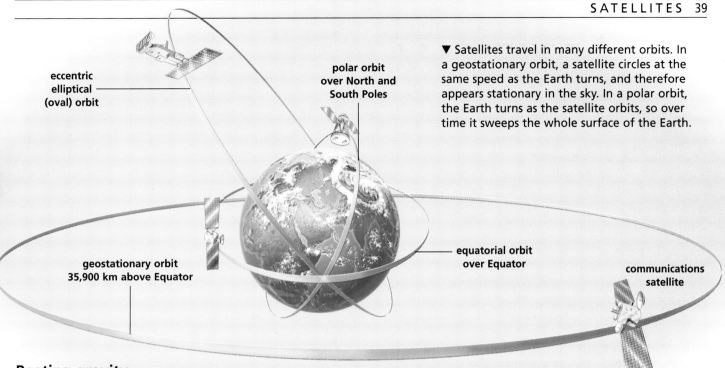

eccentric
elliptical
(oval) orbit

polar orbit
over North and
South Poles

geostationary orbit
35,900 km above Equator

equatorial orbit
over Equator

communications
satellite

▼ Satellites travel in many different orbits. In a geostationary orbit, a satellite circles at the same speed as the Earth turns, and therefore appears stationary in the sky. In a polar orbit, the Earth turns as the satellite orbits, so over time it sweeps the whole surface of the Earth.

Beating gravity

To launch things into space, we must somehow overcome gravity, the powerful pull of the Earth. How do we do this? We can get a clue by throwing a ball. If we throw the ball gently parallel with the ground, it travels only a little way before it falls down under the pull of gravity. But the faster we throw it, the farther it travels before it falls back to the ground.

If we could throw the ball at a speed of 28,000 kilometres an hour, a strange thing would happen. It would fall at the same rate as the Earth curves. In other words, it would stay the same height above the Earth. It would become a satellite of the Earth.

Real satellites have to be launched from the Earth at this very high speed, which is called the orbital velocity. To reach such a speed, satellites have to be launched by powerful rockets. Rockets are the only engines that can work in space.

What satellites are like

Satellites are built from light but strong materials. They come in many shapes and sizes. For example, the scientific satellite *Lageos* is a sphere only about 60 centimetres across. However, the Hubble Space Telescope is more than 13 metres long and weighs 11 tonnes.

Satellites carry all kinds of equipment – instruments to measure different kinds of radiation, other instruments to measure magnetism, telescopes, cameras and a radio. The radio sends the information and pictures from all the other equipment back to a control centre, or ground station, back on Earth.

All the equipment on satellites works by electricity, usually produced by solar cells. These are batteries that work by sunlight. The panels you see on many satellites are made up of thousands of solar cells.

key words

- gravity
- orbit
- orbital velocity
- rocket
- solar cell

◄ This dish aerial on the ground sends and receives radio signals to and from a communications satellite in orbit high above. Intelsat, the world's biggest communications satellite network, uses ground stations in over 100 countries to pass on communications around the world.

JOURNEY INTO SPACE

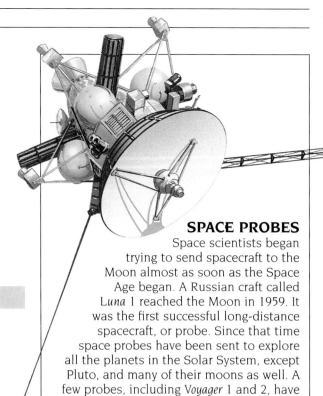

On 12 April 1961, Russian pilot Yuri Gagarin became the fastest man alive. Travelling at a speed of nearly 8 kilometres per second, he rocketed into orbit to become the first man in space. He said afterwards, 'The rocket engines were creating the music of the future.'

A Russian schoolteacher named Konstantin Tsiolkovsky first suggested in the early 1900s that rockets could be used for exploring outer space. But it was more than 50 years before rockets were powerful enough to launch objects into space. The first objects launched were satellites. These are spacecraft that circle round and round the Earth in orbit.

 key words

- astronaut
- cosmonaut
- space station
- spacewalk

SPACE PROBES

Space scientists began trying to send spacecraft to the Moon almost as soon as the Space Age began. A Russian craft called *Luna* 1 reached the Moon in 1959. It was the first successful long-distance spacecraft, or probe. Since that time space probes have been sent to explore all the planets in the Solar System, except Pluto, and many of their moons as well. A few probes, including *Voyager* 1 and 2, have reached the edge of the Solar System and are heading for the stars.

Human spaceflight

Before Gagarin's pioneering flight, no one knew whether humans would survive travelling in space. But we now know that they can. And they can stay in space for months at a time.

Many countries now launch satellites into space, but only two have launched people – the United States and Russia. In the United States, space activities are controlled by NASA, the National Aeronautics and Space Agency. US astronauts ride into space in the space shuttle, which has been flying since 1981. Russian cosmonauts fly into space in Soyuz spacecraft, which have been operating since 1967.

The US and Russia are working together to build an international space station in orbit, in which astronauts and cosmonauts will work. Europe is working with them through the European Space Agency (ESA). So is Japan through its space agency NASDA.

Human spaceflight is very expensive. So it seems sensible for several countries to share the costs of future missions, such as setting up bases on the Moon and Mars.

MILESTONES IN SPACE TRAVEL

1957
▶ Russia launches the first satellite, *Sputnik 1* on 4 October. *Sputnik 2*, launched a month later, carries the first space traveller, a dog called Laika.

1958
US launches its first satellite, *Explorer 1*, which discovers the Earth's Van Allen radiation belts.

1961
Yuri Gagarin (Russia) becomes the first man in space, travelling once around the Earth in a *Vostok 1* capsule on 12 April.

1969
◄ On 20 July *Apollo 11* lands on the Moon. Neil Armstrong and Buzz Aldrin (pictured here) take the first steps on the surface.

1971
Russia launches the first space station, *Salyut 1*.

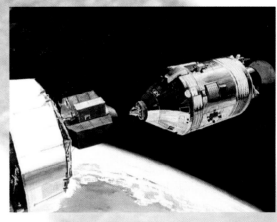

1968
Frank Borman, James Lovell and William Anders become the first humans to fly around the Moon in *Apollo 8*.

1975
▲ Apollo-Soyuz docking. US and Russia mount the first joint mission in space, the Apollo-Soyuz Test Project.

1981
On 12 April the US space shuttle makes its maiden voyage. The orbiter *Columbia* spends just over two days in space.

1965
On 18 March Alexei Leonov (Russia) makes the first spacewalk from *Voskhod 2*.

1986
On 28 January the space shuttle orbiter *Challenger* blows up shortly after lift-off, killing its crew of seven. Also in January, Russia launches the first part of its *Mir* space station.

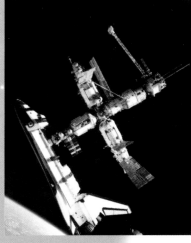

1963
▼ Valentina Tereshkova (Russia) flies in *Vostok 6*. She is the first woman to travel in space

1995
▲ First US space shuttle link-up with Russian space station *Mir*.

1998
◄ *Zarya*, the first module for the international space station (ISS), is launched by Russia.

1962
On 20 February John Glenn becomes the first American in orbit, flying in a Mercury capsule called *Friendship 7*.

2000
Astronauts live in the partly built ISS for the first time.

LIVING IN SPACE

If you were an astronaut up in space, you would find life very strange. You wouldn't be able to walk, because in space you can't keep your feet on the floor. You couldn't pour yourself a drink, because drinks don't pour in space. And you would have to sleep strapped in your bed to avoid floating away.

Astronauts are people who travel in space. The Russians call them cosmonauts. The Russian cosmonaut Yuri Gagarin became the first space traveller in 1961. Since then hundreds of astronauts and cosmonauts have flown into space – men and women, young and old, from many different countries.

Getting ready

Imagine you are an astronaut about to set out on a space mission. Before you set out, you have to train hard, rehearsing the work you will carry out in orbit. You spend a lot of time in simulators. These are machines that behave in the same way as your spacecraft without leaving the ground. You go over and over the details of your trip with mission control, the centre that controls missions from the ground.

▶ Astronauts train for space walks (EVA) in a large water tank. This gives them the same sense of weightlessness that they will have when floating in space.

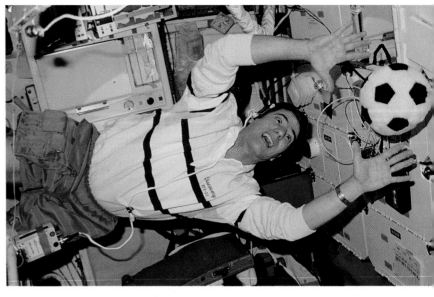

key words
- EVA
- simulators
- spacesuit
- weightlessness

▲ An astronaut 'goalkeeper' appears to dive to catch a ball. But he's just kidding. Both he and the ball are floating motionless in space.

Into orbit

When it is time for the launch, you strap yourself into your seat, facing away from the ground. As the launch rockets fire, you feel yourself flattened against the seat. Your body feels much heavier than usual. This is because of the forces set up as the rocket accelerates. They are called g-forces, the g standing for gravity.

Floating free

Once the rockets stop firing and you are circling the Earth in orbit, your body no longer feels heavy. If you unstrap yourself, you float gently out of your seat. It appears that your body has no weight at all! We call this peculiar state zero-g, or weightlessness.

Weightlessness affects everything you do in orbit. It's best not to eat crumbly foods, because the crumbs will float away and get into everything. You have to drink liquids through a straw because there is no gravity to make them pour. Even the lavatory you use in space has to be flushed with air, rather than water.

Russian cosmonaut Valery Polyakov holds the record for the longest stay in space. He spent over 437 days in orbit in the Mir space station, between January 1994 and March 1995.

Space medicine

Weightlessness not only affects the way you behave in orbit, it also upsets your body. It affects the balance organs in your ears, and this could make you feel travel sick for a while. Your face will get fatter, but your waist will get slimmer and you will grow a few centimetres taller.

 If you stay in space for a long time, the effects of weightlessness are more serious. Because your muscles no longer have to battle against gravity, they get flabby and start to waste away. To keep them in good shape you will need to exercise regularly. You might jog on a treadmill, or ride on a bicycle machine. Because the effects of long stays in space can be serious, astronauts take part in medical experiments to see how weightlessness affects their bodies.

Walking in space

While you are in orbit, you might have to go on a spacewalk. The correct term for a spacewalk is extravehicular activity, or EVA.

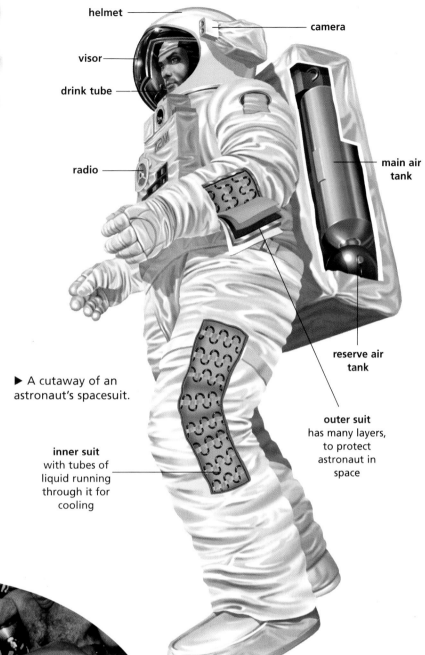

helmet
camera
visor
drink tube
radio
main air tank
reserve air tank
outer suit has many layers, to protect astronaut in space
inner suit with tubes of liquid running through it for cooling

▶ A cutaway of an astronaut's spacesuit.

To go outside the spacecraft you will need a spacesuit. This gives you air to breathe and protects you from the heat, cold and dangerous radiation of space. You may also have a backpack with small jets on it to help you move about.

◀ An astronaut takes part in a medical experiment to check on her breathing and circulation. Such experiments are vital for the long-term future of human beings in space.

SHUTTLING INTO ORBIT

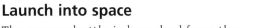

The space shuttle is part rocket, part spacecraft and part aircraft. It blasts off the launch pad like a rocket. It manoeuvres in orbit like a spacecraft. And it glides into land like an aircraft. Unlike other rockets, the shuttle can be used over and over again.

The space shuttle has been carrying astronauts into space since 1981. There have been over 100 shuttle flights since then. The shuttle's payload bay (cargo area) can carry satellites such as the Hubble Space Telescope into orbit. It is also used to carry parts of the International Space Station. The cargo bay can also house Spacelab, a complete laboratory where scientists can carry out experiments.

Launch into space

The space shuttle is launched from the Kennedy Space Center in Florida, USA. On the launch pad, the orbiter is mounted on two solid rocket boosters (SRBs) and a huge external fuel tank. On lift-off, the orbiter's main engines and the SRBs all fire at once. Together they have the power of a whole fleet of jumbo jet airliners.

▶ The orbiter *Endeavour* releases a braking parachute after it has touched down on the runway. *Endeavour* is one of four orbiters in operation. The others are *Columbia*, *Atlantis* and *Discovery*.

key words
- boosters
- drag
- orbiter
- re-entry

As the orbiter climbs into space, the SRBs and the external tank fall away in turn as their fuel is used up. The SRBs are recovered, but the tank is not.

Down to Earth

At the end of its mission, the orbiter re-enters the Earth's atmosphere, travelling very fast. Air resistance slows the orbiter down, but at the same time makes it heat up because of friction. To keep out the heat, the orbiter is covered with insulation.

About 25 minutes after re-entry, the orbiter glides in to land at Kennedy Space Center.

▶ Diagram of the shuttle orbiter showing a satellite being placed in Earth orbit. The shuttle has a long robot arm, which it can use to launch and also capture satellites.

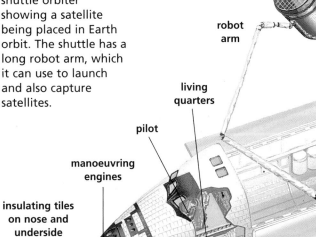

satellite

robot arm

living quarters

pilot

manoeuvring engines

insulating tiles on nose and underside

payload bay

ma...
eng...

HOMES IN SPACE

 Later this century, you could be living and working on a huge space station, watching the Sun rise and set 16 times a day. From there, you might catch a lunar ferry that would whisk you to a base on the Moon, or a spaceship heading for the planet Mars.

Space stations are spacecraft in which astronauts stay in space for a long time. They circle in orbit around the Earth a few hundred kilometres high.

Russia has launched a number of space stations, including Mir, launched in 1986. The United States launched the space station Skylab in 1973. Mir has been the most successful, with astronauts, cosmonauts and scientists from many countries visiting to live and carry out experiments in space.

key words
- module
- orbit

▲ *Mir* in orbit, photographed by astronauts in a visiting space shuttle. It is made up of a number of parts, or modules. They were launched one by one and put together in orbit. The flat panels that look like windmill sails are solar panels, which convert sunlight into electric power.

The ISS

Today, Russia and the United States are working together with Europe, Japan and Canada on the construction of a large international space station, the ISS.

The ISS is being built bit by bit. Each piece, or module, is carried into orbit, and linked up to modules already there. A Russian Proton rocket carried the first module, named *Zarya*, into orbit in November 1998. Among the other modules of the station are a Russian service module (*Zvezda*), a living quarters, and several laboratories.

In time, the ISS, or a space station like it, may be expanded to become a port for spacecraft, travelling to the Moon and eventually to Mars.

▶ An artist's impression of what the completed international space station will look like. It will be more than 100 m long and weigh about 400 tonnes.

GLOSSARY

The glossary gives simple explanations of difficult or specialist words that readers might be unfamiliar with. Words in *italic* have their own glossary entry.

aerofoil The shape of aircraft wings or helicopter rotor blades, which gives them lift.

alloy A metal formed by mixing two or more metals together. For example, brass is an alloy of copper and zinc.

alternative energy Energy produced from renewable natural sources, such as the Sun, wind, flowing water and waves.

automation The use of automatic machines, often under computer control, to do jobs.

email (electronic mail) Messages sent between computers, usually via the internet.

genetic engineering The science of altering or transplanting genes to produce new organisms.

gravity The natural force that pulls everything towards the Earth.

hydraulic power A power source that uses the pressure of liquid.

hydroelectric power Electricity that is made using the energy of running water.

locomotive The engine or power unit of a train.

machine tools Machines that are used to cut and shape metal. They are very accurate and can make many identical parts.

machining A metal-shaping process carried out by *machine tools* such as lathes and milling machines.

laser (Light Amplification by Stimulated Emission of Radiation) A device that produces a thin, bright beam of light.

mass production Manufacturing products in large quantities, using machines.

microchip A wafer-thin sliver of crystal (usually silicon) that carries miniature electronic circuits.

module A self-contained unit, particularly of a spacecraft.

nuclear power Power that comes from the nuclei of atoms.

orbit The path one object takes around another, especially the path taken by something moving round a planet or other body in space.

pollution The poisoning of the environment by such things as oil, chemicals and car exhaust fumes.

probe A spacecraft that journeys deep into space to explore planets, moons and asteroids.

radar A navigation aid that detects objects by bouncing radio waves off them.

recycling Using the same materials again, either for the same or a different purpose, to help save materials. For example, waste paper can be recycled to make cardboard, and broken glass can be melted with other ingredients to make new glass.

robot An automatic machine, particularly one that carries out similar tasks to humans.

satellite A small object in orbit around a larger one, for example a spacecraft *orbiting* the Earth.

simulator A dummy machine that simulates, or works in the same way as, a real one. For example, an aircraft simulator is used by pilots to practise flying.

solar cell A crystal device that converts solar energy directly into electricity. Solar cells are used to power things like pocket calculators and satellites.

solar power Power made using energy from the Sun, which can be used for such purposes as heating water.

sonar A method of navigation that finds objects under water by bouncing sound waves off them.

streamlined An object that is carefully shaped and smooth so that it can move more easily through air or water.

supersonic Travelling at speeds greater than the speed of sound.

technology The use of science in everyday life and in industry.

turbine A machine or motor driven by a flow of water, steam or gas.

wind tunnel A device that blows air past models of aircraft, vehicles and structures. It gives engineers an idea of how the real objects will behave when they are in use.

INDEX

Page numbers in **bold** mean that this is where you will find the most information on that subject. If both a heading and a page number are in bold, there is an article with that title. A page number in *italic* means that there is a picture of that subject. There may also be other information about the subject on the same page.

ACKNOWLEDGEMENTS

Key
t = top; c = centre; b = bottom; r = right; l = left;
back = background; fore = foreground.

Artwork
Baum, Julian: 38 tl; 40 c; 42 tr; 44 tl. **Birkett,
Georgie:** 24 tl. **Bull, Peter:** 14 tr. **Hardy, David:** 36 tr.
Hawken, Nick: 40 tr; 44 b. **Oxford Illustrators:** 13 t;
27 b; 42 tl. **Parsley, Helen:** 13 b. **Polley, Robbie:** 18
tr. **Sarson, Peter:** 6 b; 15 tr; 38 c. **Sarson, Peter
/Julian Baker:** 7 t; 35 c; 39 t. **Saunders, Mike:** 15 b;
16 c; 21 b; 22 r; 23 b; 28 b; 32–33 b; 34–35 b.
Visscher, Peter: 4 tl; 6 tl; 8 tl; 10 tl; 11 tl; 12 tl; 14
tl; 16 tl; 18 tl; 20 tl; 21 tl; 22 tl; 23 tl; 26 tl; 27 tl;
29 tl, b; 31 tl, tr; 34 tl; 36 tl; 40 tl; 45 tl, b. **Woods,
Michael:** 11 b.

Photos
*The publishers would like to thank the following
for permission to use their photographs.*

Courtesy of AGCO Corporation: 10 b; 12 bl.

BAE Systems: 31 tl.

Breitling SA: 31 b (Jean-Francois Luy).

Bridgeman Art Library: 8 br (Private Collection).

Corbis: 6 tr (Archivo Iconografico, S.A.); 10 tr (Jack
Fields); 17 t (Michael S. Yamashita); 19 bl (Adam
Woolfitt); 18 br (Joel W. Rogers); 20 bl (Tony
Arruza); 26 tr (Roger Antrobus); 27 tr (Tim Wright);
28 tr (Kelly Harriger); 29 tr (Colin Garratt; Milepost
921/2); 33 tr (Galen Rowell); 35 tr (Chris North;
Cordaiy Photo Library Ltd.).

Digital Vision: 8 tr; 9 bl; 16 tr; 21 tr; 30 b; 34 tr.
IBM: 4 tr.

MVP, Munich: 30 tr.

NASA: 41 tl, tr, cr, b; 43 tr, b; 44 tr; 45 tr, b.
Novosti (London): 40 br; **Science Photo Library:** 15
cr (US Navy); 22 bl (David Parker); 36 bl (Philippe
Plailly); 37 bl (Peter Menzel); 41 bl (Novosti); 42 b
(Novosti).

Space Charts Photo Library: 23 tr; 38 c, bl; 39 br.
Courtesy of Specialized Bicycles: 26 b.
The Aviation Picture Library: 14 bl (Aerospatiale-
Missiles/ADIP).

The British Library: 12 tr.

TRH Pictures: 7 bl (BAE).